Being in a GANG

Stories from Survivors

SARAH EASON AND KAREN LATCHANA KENNEY

CHERITON
CHILDREN'S BOOKS

Please visit our website, www.cheritonchildrensbooks.com to see more of our high-quality books.

First Edition

Published in 2022 by Cheriton Children's Books
PO Box 7258, Bridgnorth, Shropshire, WV16 9ET, UK

© 2022 Cheriton Children's Books

Authors: Sarah Eason and Karen Latchana Kenney
Designer: Paul Myerscough
Illustrator: Sylwia Filipczak
Editor: Jennifer Sanderson
Picture Researcher: Rachel Blount
Proofreader: Tracey Kelly

Printed in the United States of America

Publisher's Note: The stories in this book are fictional stories based on extensive research of real-life experiences.

CONTENTS

CHAPTER ONE

WHEN A PERSON JOINS A GANG

Around the world, gangs are a huge problem and one that is growing all the time. There are approximately 1 million gang members in the United States. There are around 20,000 organized gangs, all operating throughout the country. These gangs devastate their communities and cause particular harm to the young people whom they attract as members. It is a harsh statistic that young people who are members of gangs die every day.

WHAT ARE GANGS?

Gangs are large, organized groups of people who have a common purpose. They may participate in criminal activities, such as drug dealing or gun violence, and most often, they claim power over certain areas of communities. To show members' **affiliation** to a specific gang, they may wear a common color or have a sign or symbol and name. Gangs are found in all social and **ethnic** groups. Although most gang members are male, more and more female members are joining gangs. Many gangs **recruit** members at a young age and have leaders that direct the gang's operations.

Being in a gang can make young people feel part of something bigger than themselves.

WHY DO PEOPLE BECOME PART OF A GANG?

Gangs have been around for many years, and they form in all kinds of communities. For vulnerable teenagers, gangs offer a type of family. They make young people feel like they belong and are loved. At the same time, the gang protects young people from **rival** gangs in dangerous neighborhoods. Teens may feel that they have a purpose in a gang, especially in communities that lack opportunities and are rundown. However, the gang "family" can lead teens to crime, especially violent gun crimes and **drug abuse**. In many cases, belonging to a gang means an early death.

Gangs often seek out young people who are vulnerable and looking for support.

It Happened to Me

This book follows the "It Happened to Me" fictional journals of different young people who have become involved with gangs. These stories from survivors explain how they became part of a gang, and what it is like to be in a gang. The conclusions to their stories on pages 44-45 also show that it is possible to escape gangs and lead a happy and fulfilling life. The stories and information in this book can support people who are involved with gangs and help everyone better understand what it is like to be in this situation.

TYPES OF GANGS

Not all gangs are the same, but they are all very complex groups. Some operate on a national level. Others are much smaller and can be found only in a certain local area. The membership of each gang varies, too. Gangs may include members of just one ethnic group, or only males or females. They can be more **diverse**, depending on their location and purpose.

CRIMINAL GANGS

Many gangs are heavily involved with crime. There are three main types of criminal gang:

- *Street Gangs*: Street gangs operate in a city, suburb, or **rural** area. They are the type found in most parts of the United States. As their name suggests, they form on the street and each gang controls a certain **territory**. Some street gangs are part of a larger national group. Others are localized and can be found only in one area of a city.
- *Prison Gangs*: This gang type forms inside the **penal system** across the United States. The members are prisoners, who operate from within a prison where the criminal activity takes place.
- *Outlaw Motorcycle Gangs*: An outlaw motorcycle gang (OMG) is made up of motorcycle club members that use their motorcycle club to conduct criminal activity. Some OMGs are called "One Percenters." This comes from a statement made in the 1960s that 99 percent of motorcyclists were law-abiding citizens. OMG members promise to use violence and act in criminal ways.

Gang activity is a big problem in American prisons.

Gang activity is far more likely to take place in rundown areas than in wealthier neighborhoods. This is because having little to occupy a person's time can easily lead to gang involvement.

OTHER GANGS

There are also hybrid gangs, hate groups, and occult groups. All of these gangs use violence in different ways. Hybrid gangs are local gangs with less structure than most street gangs. A hate group is a gang of people who have a shared hatred of another group. An occult group may practice **satanic** worship or heavily use drugs.

"Joining a street gang made me feel safe—like they had my back."

IT HAPPENS

There are hundreds of groups operating in different states under the same main gang names. Some of these national gangs are very well known, including the Latin Kings, the Bloods, Crips, and the Black Gangster Disciples. The Latin Kings is the largest Hispanic gang in the United States—with more than 30,000 members. It is found in 34 US states, as well as having a presence in Canada, Ecuador, Italy, and Spain. The Bloods and the Crips are two rival gangs that started in Los Angeles in the 1960s but have since spread across the country. The Bloods are known by their red bandannas or clothing, while blue is the color of the Crips. The Black Gangster Disciples is an African-American gang that is heavily involved with dealing drugs. It is known to be very violent.

GANGS ON THE STREET

Street gangs can be found in almost every part of the United States —from rural areas to towns and cities. However, the spread of the problem varies widely, depending on the type of area the gang operates in. Approximately 41 percent of all US gangs are found in larger cities, and 31 percent are in smaller cities. Suburban counties are where just over 23 percent of the gangs are found, while rural counties contain fewer than 5 percent.

GANGS IN THE COMMUNITY

There are certain factors in communities that encourage gang formation. Gangs usually take root in areas that are **socially disadvantaged** and that have high crime rates. This means that there may be poverty, unemployment, and single-parent households with many children in those homes. In these areas, there are often problems within families, and there may be poor education systems in which many teens drop out of school. As a result of these factors, there is often not enough adult

Rundown neighborhoods are often breeding grounds for gangs and gang crime.

According to a National Youth Gang Survey, 2 out of every 5 gang members are under the age of 18. That's about 35 percent of all gang members.

Having no work and nothing to do can easily lead to gang involvement.

supervision. Sometimes, the only parent present may have to work long hours to support the family. Other times, an elderly grandparent may take care of the children in a family. They may feel overwhelmed and be unable to care for them properly. This can leave teenagers with a lot of free time without adults watching them.

NOT ENOUGH JOBS

In socially disadvantaged areas, there are also often few career or job opportunities. Teens who have dropped out of school lack the education to find employment or make money. This makes working for a gang and earning cash even more appealing. For gangs to form, there needs to be a place where large groups of people can meet. This is usually in a defined neighborhood.

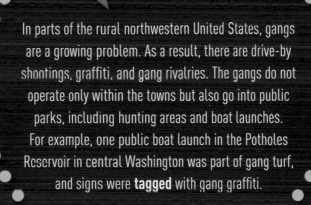

IT HAPPENS

In parts of the rural northwestern United States, gangs are a growing problem. As a result, there are drive-by shootings, graffiti, and gang rivalries. The gangs do not operate only within the towns but also go into public parks, including hunting areas and boat launches. For example, one public boat launch in the Potholes Reservoir in central Washington was part of gang turf, and signs were **tagged** with gang graffiti.

I Wish I Could Tell Mom

FRIDAY APRIL 23

I hate being at home. Mom is always working since Dad left, and I have to take care of Julie all the time, my dumb little sister. I told Sharlene how lame it was at school today. She laughed and said there's no way she'd do it. She told me to start coming out and hanging out with her and her friends. She says she's part of a really cool gang.

I thought Todd was cute at first, now I'm really scared of him.

SUNDAY MAY 16

I went out with Sharlene this weekend. It was so fun! We went to the mall, with a whole gang of other kids. I don't really know them well, but they were really cool. They bought me loads of stuff—I couldn't believe it! Sharlene says I should come again. She says one of the guys, Todd, says I can hang with them. Mom was mad at me for leaving Julie alone for so long. I don't care—it's not my fault she has to work all the time. I'm not Julie's mom, why should I have to take care of her?

WEDNESDAY JUNE 9

After school, I met up with Sharlene, Todd, and the other guys at the beach. Todd told me he really likes me, and he wants me to be part of the gang for good. He asked me if I want to join. I said yes. I really like him. Sharlene said maybe he will be my boyfriend—I'd love that!

FRIDAY JULY 16

Todd kissed me today. Then he said if I want to be his girl, I need to do whatever he says. That made me feel weird, a bit scared. He told me I need to take care of something for him. I freaked out when he pulled out a gun. He said he needs me to hide it at home. I told him I didn't want to do it. He got really mean then. He pushed me up against a wall and told me if I don't do it, he'll tell the other girls in the gang, and they'll beat me up. I was really scared. Todd says I've got a couple of days to decide what to do, that he's going easy on me as a favor. I wish I could tell Mom what's going on, but I'm too scared Todd will find out ...

CHAPTER TWO

HOW TEENS GET INTO GANGS

To high school dropouts, joining a gang may seem like a solution to all their problems. These young people have little chance of further education, limited finances, and scant support from family. Gangs can offer them an **identity.** They also offer a feeling of power. Many vulnerable teens find the attraction of gangs impossible to resist.

DROPPING OUT

While anyone can join a gang, a typical gang recruit is a teenage boy or young adult who has dropped out of high school. They usually have no employment prospects, a history of difficulties with the law, and little family support. A recruit may also have a lot of free time with little to do, and they may feel badly about the direction in which their life is going.

Close friendships and being part of a group are normal and healthy for young people. The problems come when they are drawn toward a gang.

Gangs can offer them an identity.

Teenagers who have little family support will find being part of a gang appealing.

TEENS DRAWN IN

There are many reasons why gang life may be attractive to the typical recruit. In dangerous neighborhoods, a gang can offer a teenager protection because the members look out for each other. Being associated with a gang can also be a way for teens to survive the tough streets of their neighborhood. Gangs may make teens feel empowered. Teenagers believe that being a gang member will make others respect and even fear them. Gangs may also provide a place where the teen can feel like they belong. For a teen who feels like a misfit, a gang family can become home, with gang members becoming the teen's "brothers and sisters." Gang members socialize together, have parties, and drink alcohol. They may also take illegal drugs. All of these activities can be very appealing to teenagers. Teens may also see that their friends are joining gangs and feel enormous **peer** pressure to join, too.

Gangs use the Internet to recruit new members. They post content on social media sites that makes gang life look glamorous. They also boast about what they have done.

Fighting is a skill that most gangs value.

GANG INITIATIONS

To become a gang member, recruits must be initiated, or formally made a member. Most gangs have a distinct initiation ceremony. There are different kinds of initiation, and some are more violent than others. Here are examples of the most common types:

- **Rolled or Jumped In**: This is when a recruit must fight other gang members for a certain period of time. The recruit must show that they can take the beating. That is because gang members want to see if the recruit is a tough person and a good fighter.
- **Lined In**: During this initiation ceremony, gang members stand in two lines. The recruit has to move down the middle of the lines while being beaten.
- **Sexed In**: This initiation is used for female recruits to mostly male gangs. It requires them to have sex with several male gang members.
- **Jacked In**: For this initiation, recruits must commit a crime. For example, they may be expected to rob a house or steal a car.
- **Blood In**: There are two ways for a blood in to happen. Sometimes, a recruit may have to be beaten until they bleed. Other times, a recruit has to murder someone.
- **Courted In**: In this situation, a recruit is simply asked to join the gang. They do not have to go through a violent initiation ceremony. This is usually because the gang wants the talents, skills, or connections that the recruit has.

In 2021 in Chicago, between the Father's Day and Fourth of July weekends, 416 people were shot in gang-related violence, and 74 of those people died as a result.

IT HAPPENS

The Covid-19 pandemic has dramatically affected gang activity. From 2020, police forces across the country have documented a marked increase in gang activity, particularly among adolescents. The increase has been linked directly to the closure of schools and after-school activities for young people. Without the structure of in-school education and the support network of teachers, social workers, and activity leaders, young people are far more vulnerable to gang recruitment. Gang-related shootings and stabbings have soared, and cities across the country have seen a significant rise in deaths caused by gang violence.

BRUTAL OUTCOMES

Initiation can be brutal and extremely violent, and as a result, recruits may die. If recruits are sexed in, they can contract **sexually transmitted diseases** such as the human immunodeficiency virus (HIV), or they may become pregnant.

Initiation into a gang can be very disturbing for young people.

This Is Easy Money

MONDAY JUNE 7

Dad has been yelling at me again today about getting a job. He says I quit school, so now I can bring in some money. I told him I've been looking, but there are no jobs around here—he should know, he's been out of work for years. But Dad just yelled at me and said I can't stay here unless I pull my weight.

WEDNESDAY SEPTEMBER 15

I caught up with Ben today. He saw me in town and called me over. He was with a group of other kids, just hanging out. Luke, my brother, says they are bad news, and I should stay away from them. But they seemed OK to me. We went to the skate park. Ben said, watch this, and went over to one of the schoolkids. Couldn't believe it—this guy bought a package of **coke** from Ben. Easy money, Ben said, you should try it. He had a fistful of dollars. It made me feel good, hanging out with Ben and the other guys. Like I was part of something, kind of like a family. Better than the one back home.

SUNDAY OCTOBER 10

I've made more money this week than I'd make in any job! Ben was right, this is easy money. I've been selling coke and other drugs at the skate park. Cashing in on the rich high school kids! I gave Dad my share for the bills. He looked surprised and said, where did you get that? I told him, I'm earning. He just shrugged and told me to make sure I keep it coming.

I can't see any future around here. The gang is all I have.

THURSDAY FEBRUARY 10

Ben said some other kids are trying to push in on our area. He said they are dealing at the park and taking our business. We went down to the park with the other guys. Ben was right. Another gang was there, selling. Ben told me we had to protect our patch. I knew I was going to have to fight—all the guys were moving in, ready to go. I didn't see it coming, though. Next thing I knew, my leg was bleeding, really bad. Ben started yelling. I can't remember much after that ...

CHAPTER THREE

HOW GANGS WORK

Street gangs are highly organized groups that have a set of laws that members must obey. Within each gang, different members have specific roles. These are organized according to the **status** the gang member has within the group. Most gangs have a strict **hierarchy**.

GANGS WHO'S WHO

New recruits start at the bottom of the gang's structure. They have the lowest status and must do the toughest jobs. New recruits carry out the orders given by higher-ranking gang members. Usually, new members must handle the risky assignments, such as carrying the gang's drugs or guns. Higher up the hierarchy are the hard-core members. They have usually been in the gang for a while, are older, and have proven their loyalty to the gang. They are also usually the most violent of the gang's members. At the top of the organization are the gang's leaders. Gang leaders make the final decisions on any matters that impact the gang.

Some gang members have more violent roles than others.

"They told me I had to start at the bottom— and learn to toughen up."

Human trafficking, or the selling of people into slavery or prostitution, is big business for many gangs.

For example, they decide what types of criminal activity the gang is involved with. Sometimes, gang leaders direct their gangs from prison, giving their commands through phone calls or visitors.

BREAKING THE LAW

Gangs may be involved in many types of crimes. Some might be minor, but many are serious. In acts of vandalism, members may use spray paint to tag buildings, bridges, and signs, leaving their gang's symbol or messages for others. Although vandalism is against the law, it does not usually involve violence. However, most gangs are involved with violent crime. They may use high-powered guns to intimidate, or frighten, other gangs, shooting people who obstruct them. Many gangs also sell illegal drugs locally and transport drugs across the country. Some are involved in human trafficking.

Most violent crime is gang related. According to a survey by the National Gang Intelligence Center (NGIC), big cities and suburban counties see the worst gang violence. In some areas, gangs commit 48 percent of violent crimes. In other areas, this increases to 90 percent.

GANG SIGNS AND SYMBOLS

Each gang has a unique way to identify its members or crew. Symbols and signs show others which gang a person is affiliated to. Gang members use codes to communicate and different clothing and colors help identify gang members:

- *Graffiti*: Made using spray paint, graffiti are marks put on a building, sign, or structure. However, not all graffiti are gang related. Some are a symbol of hip-hop culture. Others are very artistic, with large murals showing beautiful images. Gang graffiti, which is also called tagging, are not art but instead are used to mark territory. They make people afraid by showing words or symbols. For example, a grouping of four dots is a symbol of the Norteno gang in Sacramento.

IT HAPPENS

Parents and carers of young people who have become involved with gangs have successfully broken the link with the gang by recognizing the signs of gang involvement early, from tagging to gang-related clothing. They then apply tactics such as:

- Not allowing the wearing of gang-related clothing or the use of gang-related signs, symbols, and tattoos.
  - Banning the use of graffiti art and tagging.
- Actively encouraging teens to engage in extracurricular activities such as after-school programs. These might include athletics, artistic projects, or religious groups. All provide a healthy alternative to gang culture.

Gang members use codes to communicate ...

- *Tattoos*: A tattoo is another gang symbol that shows others what gang a person is affiliated to and their commitment to that gang. Gang members get tattoos on different parts of their bodies such as on the face, neck, chest, and hands. The tattoos can sometimes show letters that symbolize or represent the gang, for example, ESL for East Side Locos in Idaho. They can also show numbers and/or a picture.
- *Colors and Clothing*: Different colors, clothing brands, and sports logos show a person's link to a gang. The Crips use the colors blue and black as their symbol, for example, and can be worn as hats or bandannas. Some Hispanic gangs wear a particular kind of outfit, with white T-shirts, baggy pants, and thin belts.
- *Hand Symbols*: Most gangs use hand symbols to communicate what gang they belong to and to threaten another person or rival gang member. The symbols represent numbers, letters, or gang names.

Hand symbols tell others what gang a person belongs to.

Gang tattoos can also be used as a form of punishment. Punishment tattoos are often given forcibly and somewhere highly visible and impossible to hide, such as the gang member's face.

NOT JUST BOYS

Although men run most gangs, females can be members, too. There are also all-female gangs made up of tough and violent girls who are comfortable with using guns and knives against rival gangs, regardless of the rivals' gender. According to the Department of Justice, there are 60,000 to 80,000 female gang members in the United States. In Los Angeles, there are around 5,000 women gangsters. All-female gangs make up 2 percent of all US gangs.

A HIDDEN THREAT

Law enforcement agencies and members of rival gangs often overlook girls, who can usually get away with more violence than their male counterparts. Girls may be drawn to gangs for the sense of power gang life gives them. Like the male gang members, many of these young women come from broken homes and find new families in gangs. Love also pulls women into gangs, and they might become involved with a gang because their boyfriend is affiliated to it.

Most people think of gangs as groups of young males who hang out together. However, girls can be part of the picture, too.

Female gang members often hide the guns and drugs of male gang members.

IT HAPPENED TO THEM

Gakirah Barnes has become one of the most famous female gang members in the United States. Gakirah grew up in Chicago and became part of a gang called the Gangster Disciples. During her time with the gang, she claimed to have killed 17 people and bragged about her killings on social media. Then, in 2014, Gakirah was shot dead—the gangster killer had become another victim of gang crime. Her story has since been made into a movie titled *Secret Life of a Gang Girl*.

ROLES FOR WOMEN

There are several different roles for women in gangs. They hide drugs or guns when needed by the male gang members, they may deal in drugs, and they may even use weapons to kill. Female gang members may also have to use their bodies and sex to get what the gang wants. For example, some women may be expected to lure men from rival gangs into traps where the men can be killed or beaten. Sometimes, a female gang member may have to pretend to like a specific man to **infiltrate** and spy on a rival gang. If a woman wants to leave a gang, she may have to be beaten or kill somebody, just like the men. However, pregnant women are usually allowed to leave a gang without committing any violence.

According to one report, female gang members are sometimes forced to have sex to settle drug debts.

The Only Family I Have Is Here

MONDAY AUGUST 9

It's been three months since I came to the **correctional facility**. In some ways, my life is easier in here than it was outside. I keep remembering the day Mom died, when I was 12, and how I've lived in one kids' home after another since. And each one was bad. I was thinking today, the only family I had after Mom went were other kids like me. No one wanted us, so we helped each other. People said we were bad because we were in gangs. But that was how we survived. We hardly went to school —what was the point? We just hung out on the streets. And that's when I started getting in trouble with the police.

Being in a gang is all I've ever known—it's all I've ever belonged to.

WEDNESDAY SEPTEMBER 8

We were all laughing today about our **convictions**. I told the other girls that the judge had convicted me for **truancy** and **curfew violation**. He said I had to go to a correctional facility because I needed to be in a safe place where I could learn. I'm learning alright! As soon as I got in here, I could see how things worked. There are as many gangs in here as there were out on the streets. And the gangs control the facility—if you want anything, you have to go through them. The facility guards know it—they just won't say it.

SUNDAY OCTOBER 10

Today, there was a fight. Danni won, of course. Her gang controls everything. Danni says she is going to watch out for me, and I can help her out, too. She says I can be part of her family. Danni is like me. Her mom and dad died when she was little, and she's been in homes, too. Danni says the system is against girls like us, and we have to stick together.

MONDAY NOVEMBER 1

I had my review today. I have three more months to go now. They've told me I need to keep out of trouble—and to stay away from Danni. She laughed when I told her! Danni says don't worry, and I'll get out, no trouble. I said to her, there is nothing for me outside, though. Being in here, being with Danni, feels safe. I'm scared about what it will be like once I leave. Where will I go? The only family I have is here ...

CHAPTER FOUR

GETTING INTO DEEPER TROUBLE

For a gang member, a firearm is a source of power because it can make others fearful. In gangs, guns command respect, and they give members the ability to commit crimes, threaten others, and protect themselves against other gangs who are also armed. With their guns, gang members may commit many different crimes and take part in gang wars and shoot-outs.

Damaging personal property, such as cars, is a large part of gang behavior.

"When I held that gun, I felt like I could do anything."

26

Gangs often steal cars, use them for criminal activity, and then burn the vehicles to destroy any evidence.

GANG CRIME

The National Youth Gang Survey reports on gang-related crimes. In a recent survey, it reported that property crime, which involves stealing or vandalizing property such as a car or a house, increased by just over 51 percent from the previous year. The survey also reported that violent crimes, such as murder and shootings, had the second-biggest increase of 48 percent. Drug sales increased by almost 33 percent.

The survey also found that certain factors influence gang violence. Issues around the buying and selling of illegal drugs resulted in the most violence. The second-highest factor was problems between gangs, which saw an increase in gang-on-gang violence and **retaliation**. The third-highest factor was issues related to gang members returning from prison. Crime keeps most gangs operating, and it helps members run their business of distributing, or spreading, and selling drugs.

The city of Los Angeles is often referred to as the gang capital of the United States. According to the Los Angeles Police Department (LAPD), during the last three years, there were more than 16,000 violent gang crimes in the City of Los Angeles. This included 491 homicides, almost 7,047 serious assaults, approximately 5,500 robberies, and just under 98 rapes.

Many gangs make their money by selling drugs.

THE DRAW OF MONEY

One of the main factors that attracts young people to gang life is the promise of money. For teens growing up in poverty, gangs may give the financial freedom they need. However, that money is "dirty" because it usually comes from illegal activities, such as selling illicit drugs.

THE DANGERS OF DRUGS

Street, prison, and outlaw motorcycle gangs are the main sellers of drugs in the United States. They may also smuggle drugs into the country and produce and transport drugs from state to state. Many of the drugs they trade in are hard drugs, such as crack cocaine and heroin, although most gangs also sell **marijuana**.

In El Paso, Texas, there are many gangs. It is just across the border from the town of Juarez in Mexico, so it is often used as the base for smuggling drugs from Mexico into the United States. Drugs are transported over the border or strapped to people who then walk across the border. Some gangs in El Paso also ship drugs internationally, to and from Europe and Asia.

By being the main drug suppliers and dealers, many gangs feed drug **addictions** in communities across the United States. Being addicted to drugs can destroy a person's life, and many addicts eventually lose everything—from their family's support to a job and a home.

BIG BUSINESS

Gangs can make millions of dollars each month from buying and selling drugs, illegally trading firearms, selling stolen goods, and prostitution. To hide all their profits and business dealings, gangs may own businesses, such as barbershops and music stores, through which they funnel their money. The illegal cash then looks like earnings from those businesses.

Drug addiction can ruin many people's lives.

One of the main factors that draw people to gangs is the promise of money.

SERIOUS DANGER

Being affiliated to a gang can be incredibly dangerous. Members have a high risk of death, arrest, and serving jail time. Many gang members die young or waste their youth serving prison sentences. It is a lifestyle that can, and usually does, lead to a dismal future.

Gang members are often shot at and killed by rival gang members. Their homes may also become shooting targets, putting their family at risk of being injured or even murdered. Many gang members are arrested numerous times and charged with serious offenses. With criminal records, the futures of these young people are then limited.

A gang member's home can be a target for the bullets of rival gang members.

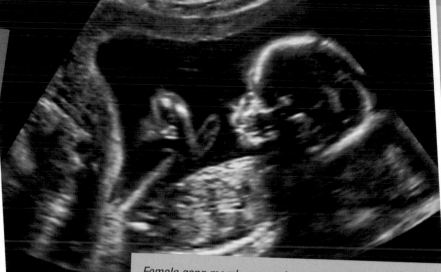

Female gang members may become pregnant after their initiation.

DROPPING OUT OF SCHOOL

Most gang recruits are high school dropouts who stop their education early and are illiterate, or unable to read and write. Before joining a gang, these recruits may have had problems finding jobs. That means that if they want to leave the gang, they must be prepared to struggle. Without a high school diploma, finding work outside of gang life is not easy, and having a criminal record can also create barriers to employment.

A HEAVY PRICE FOR GIRLS

For female gang members, early pregnancy may be a risk they take for being involved in a gang. They may become pregnant from being sexed into the gang at their initiation, or they need to get pregnant at a young age as their only way out of the gang.

A report in the *Journal of School Health* stated that drug and alcohol use was more common in schoolchildren who were gang members than it was for non-gang members. The study found that 43 percent of members were **binge drinkers**, but only 24 percent of non-gang members were binge drinkers, 54 percent of members used marijuana as opposed to 26 percent of non-gang members, and 51 percent of members sold drugs, but only 9 percent of non-gang members sold drugs.

BLIND TO THE SIGNS

Most parents do not want their teenagers to be involved with gangs. However, sometimes they just cannot see the signs of their involvement. By the time they do realize that their teenager is in a gang, it may be too late to do anything about it because their teen is already part of a gang family. That is why it is important for parents, friends, and teachers to know what signs to look for to identify if the teen is involved in gang life. If those signs are identified early enough, a teenager can be stopped from becoming a gang member.

Here are some of the early signs that a teenager is becoming involved with a gang:

- **New Friends**: A teen suddenly has new friends who seem rougher or tougher than the teen's old friends.
- **Gang Symbols**: The teen has gang symbols written on their schoolbooks, clothing, or school locker. They may also start wearing a bandanna or hat in a certain color that is usually associated with a gang in their neighborhood. Parents and teachers should also watch for tattoos or hand signals, which are used by gangs.
- **No Interest**: A teen might start skipping school or not caring about their homework or grades. The teen may stop listening to their parents and other adults, too.

Getting a tattoo can be linked to joining a gang.

IT HAPPENS

It is common to find gangs and drugs in schools. In survey by the National Center on Addiction and Substance Abuse at Columbia University (CASA), nearly one-third of children between the ages of 12 and 17 said that their schools had gang and drug problems. In fact, public schools are where gangs find most of their recruits.

- **Using Drugs and Alcohol:** The teen starts going out at night and on the weekends. They may spend most of the night out and are vague when questioned about their activities. The teen may show signs of drug and alcohol use, such as sleeping late, having mood swings, or possessing drug paraphernalia, such as a drug pipe or syringes, in their bedroom.
- **Weapons and Cash:** A teen who has large amounts of cash is likely to be involved in something that is illegal. Having weapons, such as guns or knives, is another red flag that a teen is involved with a gang.
- **Getting Arrested:** If a teen is arrested, it is important to understand what the charges are. An arrest confirms that a teen is doing something illegal.

Staying out and partying can be a sign of gang involvement.

HOW DO PEOPLE LEAVE GANGS?

Compared to joining a gang, getting out of a gang is difficult. If someone chooses to leave the gang, it can be a slow and often painful process. Sometimes, gang leaders do not let their members leave alive. After awhile, the attraction of being in a gang weakens for some people. Members may start to mature and grow out of the gang lifestyle. Some begin to have families and want to care for their partners and children by providing a good life for them away from the violence of gang life. They also may have a job and need to focus on the job's responsibilities without being distracted by the gang. Sometimes, a gang member may have had one too many deeply disturbing experiences in the gang, and that can push the person away. For example, a close friend may have been murdered in gang warfare, the violence could become too hard to take after awhile, or law enforcement agencies might be pressuring the member to leave the gang.

Once young people are part of a gang, that gang will do all it can to keep them from leaving.

When a person leaves their gang life behind, a gang tattoo is a constant reminder of their violent criminal life. A permanent inking can also prevent ex-gang members from being employed, so some **intervention programs** offer tattoo removal to help people start afresh.

GETTING OUT

Whatever the reason, just as members face initiation rituals to join a gang, getting out of the gang may require the member to become involved in some violent act. This may include murder or letting other gang members beat up the person. Sometimes, though not often, gang members can leave without any violence.

Sometimes, the only way a person can leave a gang is to kill a member of a rival gang.

"It took me years to get out of my gang—every time I tried, they'd threaten to kill me and I got too scared to leave."

I Wish He Could Get Out, Too

TUESDAY JANUARY 5

Today, I told Ethan that I wasn't into the gang anymore, that I wanted to do my own thing. I said I'd still be friends with him and the rest of the group, but I didn't want to be in on the gang stuff anymore. When Joshua was shot last month, that's when everything changed for me. Seeing that happen to him and what it did to his family—I can't put my mom and dad through that.

FRIDAY JANUARY 15

Ethan said he told Levi that I want out. Ethan said I'm lucky—Levi said he didn't care that much, that I wasn't really a big player. He says I was only on the outside of the gang, not a main man. Ethan says it's because I've never sold (drugs) for Levi, so I don't have any connections—I don't really matter to him because I'm not an earner. Ethan said it would be different for him, he's an important dealer. If he tried to leave, Levi would kill him.

Levi is older than us. He's 20. I said to Ethan, we thought he was a cool guy when he first started hanging out with us, didn't we, that he was our friend? Ethan said, yeah, remember, Levi said he could help us make money. But in the end, it's us who've been making money for him. Ethan said, now I'm stuck in it. I'll never get out.

MONDAY FEBRUARY 8

I saw Ethan and the other guys in the gang today. I've promised Mom that I won't have much to do with them, that I'll just say "Hi" if I see them. Levi was there with Ethan and the others. He just blanked me as I walked by. Ethan looked scared, like he shouldn't talk to me. I saw Levi shove him when he looked over at me. I messaged Ethan later and said, what's going on? I didn't hear back. Mom says to just leave it alone, not to get involved, but I'm worried about Ethan. He's my friend. I wish he could get out, too.

I'm lucky that I got out, but it's not going to be that easy for Ethan.

CHAPTER FIVE

PAYING THE PRICE

Gangs and gang violence and crime have serious costs to society. Some of these costs may be financial and others may cause problems for the justice and penal systems, but the worst cost of all is the many lives taken by gang violence and crime.

DRIVE-BY SHOOTINGS

A drive-by shooting is when someone drives up in a motor vehicle, shoots at a person or people, another car, or a building, and then quickly leaves the crime scene in their vehicle. The speed at which drive-by shootings occur makes it difficult for eyewitnesses to identify the criminals. Typically, in the shootings gang members fire at rivals from another gang, but innocent bystanders are often hurt or killed as they are caught in the crossfire. Sometimes, these people are not even on the street when the bullets hit them—they are inside their homes.

In areas where drive-by shootings occur frequently, community members may start to feel afraid and anxious in their own neighborhoods, and some choose not to leave their houses at night. However, even inside their houses they can be unsafe. Across the United States, news reports state that innocent children and adults are killed by stray bullets from gang members' weapons.

Every day, there is gun crime in American cities, and much of it is gang related.

Across the United States, news reports tell of innocent children and adults killed by stray bullets ...

Children playing near drive-by shootings can become the innocent victims of gang warfare.

IT HAPPENED TO THEM

Every year, innocent children die as a result of gang warfare shootings. In Columbus, Ohio, in 2020, three children were killed as a result of gang shootings in the space of just over one week. On July 22, a baby boy was killed, and his twin brother was wounded when a gang member fired shots into their home. Then, on July 25, a 14-year-old boy was shot dead when he was caught up in gang-related gunfire while riding his scooter. In the same week, another baby was killed in Akron when a gang member opened fire on his home. In 2020, in Columbus alone, a total of 13 children were killed by gang warfare.

FULL OF GANGS

Prisons in the United States are filled with gang members. Some inmates join gangs inside the prison's walls, while many belong to gangs in the outside world and continue their affiliation from inside the jails. There are high costs to keep these criminals imprisoned, and the people of the United States pay those costs. The US prison population is high—it tops 2.12 million people, which makes it the largest in the world. A high proportion of that population is gang members. In addition to the expense of keeping people in prison, if gangs operate inside prisons, members are not being **rehabilitated** during their time in jail—they just continue their gangster lifestyle while serving out their prison sentence.

US jails are filled with many gang members.

Research published in April 2020 in *The Conversation* revealed that about 10 percent of inmates in Texas prisons joined a gang for the first time in jail, while another 10 percent remained affiliated to their street gang while they were in prison. Those who joined gangs said that status and protection were the main influences for joining a prison gang.

IT HAPPENS

The Barrio Azteca is one the most violent prison gangs in the United States. Many of its 2,000 members are inside Texan prisons, but they also live in communities in Texas and New Mexico. This gang is heavily involved with drug selling and smuggling and is linked to the Mexican drug cartels, a network of criminals involved in selling and exporting illegal drugs.

A HEAVY PRICE TO PAY

It costs the United States around $81 billion each year to keep the 2.12 million people in jail, and the prisons are not succeeding in helping prisoners mend their ways. Violence is a serious problem inside jails, and when gang members are released, it is not difficult for them to go back to their old habits—around 60 percent of those who are released end up back in prison. Many states have tough sentencing laws for gang violence, which can result in sentences that are 15 years or longer—and while these sentences keep gang members off the streets, they also increase the prison costs that citizens must pay.

Youth groups provide teens with healthy environments in which to spend their spare time.

PROTECTING YOUNG PEOPLE

To keep young adults and teenagers out of gangs, prevention and education are two of the most important factors. Programs that keep teenagers off the streets after school are crucial in areas with high gang involvement because they can provide the support missing in the homes of teens vulnerable to gangs. They also simply give teenagers something constructive to do with their free time—a youth program can be the support group that teens search for in gang families. Anti-gang education is also important for both teens and their parents, because if parents know the signs of gang involvement, they can **intervene** and keep teens from being involved in gang life. Another important **deterrent** is for teens to know and understand the real consequences of gang involvement, such as death or prison time.

THE WAY OUT

There is hope, though, for those who want to escape the attraction of gangs. After-school programs can provide the support they need to stay in school and graduate. They can also provide support to teens who are vulnerable to becoming gang members and help them understand the consequences of gang life.

Parents and teachers, too, can learn the warning signs of gang involvement, so they can intervene with at-risk, vulnerable teens. Getting teens off the streets is vital because it keeps them away from the crime and violence of gangs. Programs also encourage teens to educate others about the dangers of being involved with gangs.

IT HAPPENED TO THEM

To gang and drug counselor Carlos Rodriguez, helping teens get away from gangs is his life. Rodriguez works for Omni Youth Services in a suburb of Chicago, one of the most gang-filled cities in the United States. More and more gangs are moving out from the city to the suburbs, and it was here that Rodriguez helped Ivan Ibarra escape from a gang. Rodriguez counseled Ibarra, called him often, and met him for lunch. "I found it weird," Ibarra said, "This guy was calling me and sitting down with me. We'd have interesting conversations about life, family, and culture." But the tactics worked, and after four years of working with Rodriguez, Ibarra left the gang.

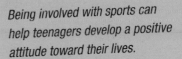

Being involved with sports can help teenagers develop a positive attitude toward their lives.

A New Start

MIA'S STORY
FRIDAY DECEMBER 10

I've been six months now since I got out of the gang. Mom says I was really lucky to get out. She says most girls don't get so lucky. It only happened because Mom read my journal. I'd written everything down about Todd, the gun, and me. Mom went crazy. I've never seen her so mad. She called the police and told them about Todd. I thought, that's it, I'm dead.

The police came over and took a statement. I cried as I told them everything. They said they had been watching Todd for awhile. Next thing I knew, Todd had been arrested—they'd caught him breaking and entering and in possession of drugs. He is in jail now. That doesn't keep me from being scared. Todd still has his gang outside, and I am on his "list." Now, Mom and I are moving. Mom says we're going to live with Grandma, so she can help take care of Julie. It will be a new start—and a new life for all of us.

BRAD'S STORY
MONDAY APRIL 18

Now it's April, and I'm getting a lot better. When I came around in the hospital, I'd lost a lot of blood. Luke said I was lucky to be alive—everyone in the gang had just run when I got shot. There was a girl in the park, though, and she called the police.

Liam: I'm still keeping my journal. I write about Ethan in it. I'll never forget him or what happened to him.

If it wasn't for her, I'd be dead. I haven't heard from Ben. Luke says I'm lucky to have gotten out of the gang, and it's my chance to turn my life around. He is joining the military next year. Luke says it's a good career and a way out of here. He says I should try it. Maybe I will.

SOFIA'S STORY
SATURDAY JUNE 11

Before I left the facility, a lady named Shelby from the reentry program visited me. She told me that the program could help me. When I left, Shelby took me to the program's house. It was OK there. Then she helped me find a job—it's not the greatest, just waitressing. But it pays the bills. Now I have moved to my own small apartment. And I've enrolled for some courses. Shelby says I need to focus on getting some qualifications, so I can get a career in the future. She asked me what I would like to do. No one has ever asked me that before! I said I didn't know, but that I liked the idea of working outdoors. Shelby said, good thinking, and let's take a look at options.

Danni has been writing to me. I did write back, but Shelby said maybe don't keep too close to Danni. Shelby says I need to focus on building up my new life and keeping away from gangs. It's hard, because I still feel alone. Shelby says I'm not on my own anymore, though, I have her now, too.

LIAM'S STORY
FRIDAY APRIL 22

It's been more than a year since I left the gang. I kept messaging Ethan, but I only heard back from him once. His message just said, leave me alone, don't contact me again. But I knew that was Levi— that he'd put Ethan up to it. Mom said I had to leave it alone, not to get involved. I'd gotten out, I was safe, that was all that matters. But I feel bad about Ethan.

MONDAY JUNE 13

I can't believe it. Ethan is dead. He got shot. Just like Joshua. Mom's been crying all week—saying all these young boys keep getting killed, and it could have been me. At first I felt numb, like it wasn't real. Now, I feel mad. This would never have happened to Ethan if he hadn't met Levi. I keep telling my little brothers, don't ever do it —never get into a gang.

45

GLOSSARY

addictions situations in which people are unable to stop using substances such as drugs and alcohol

affiliation closely associated with something or someone

binge drinkers people who drink large amounts of alcohol at one time

coke an informal word for the drug cocaine

convictions declared by a judge to be guilty of offenses

correctional facility a place where a person is kept as a punishment after they have been arrested

curfew violation breaking rules requiring a person to be indoors at a certain time

deterrent something that discourages a person from doing something

diverse including many different types, for example, people of different sexes, ethnicity, and social background

drug abuse the harmful use of drugs

ethnic relating to a population group, such as African American, Asian, Hispanic, or white

hierarchy a system in which members of a group are ranked according to their importance

identity how a person views themself

infiltrate to get into and become part of something, such as a gang

intervene to step in with the intention of changing something

intervention programs plans to stop people from doing harmful things and thereby improve their lives

marijuana a drug that can make people feel sleepy and relaxed

peer a person of a similar age

penal system the system of legal punishment

recruit to enlist new members to a group; also, a new member

rehabilitated restored to normal life

retaliation fighting back

rival a group that competes with others

rural in the countryside; away from towns and cities

satanic related to the Devil

sexually transmitted diseases diseases that are passed to other people through sexual activity

socially disadvantaged having fewer life chances because of factors such as family background, location, education, and race

status a person's position in a group

tagged marked with a graffiti sign or symbol

territory an area of land that is controlled by a person or group

truancy not attending school

FIND OUT MORE

BOOKS

Bow, James. *Gangs* (Straight Talk About ...). Crabtree Publishing, 2013.

Marty, Gitlin. *I'm Being Targeted by a Gang. Now What?* (Teen Life 411). Rosen Publishing, 2017.

Philip, Wolny. *Defeating Gangs in Your Neighborhood and Online* (Effective Survival Strategies). Rosen Publishing, 2016.

WEBSITES

Learn more about peer pressure and how to say "no" at:
kidshealth.org/en/teens/peer-pressure.html?ref=search

Find out more about gangs at:
nationalgangcenter.ojp.gov/about/faq

Learn about preventing gang membership at:
nlj.ojp.gov/topics/articles/changing-course-preventing-gang-membership

ORGANIZATIONS

Grasp/Gang Rescue and Support Project
1625 E. 35th Ave
Denver, CO 80205
(303) 777-3117
Website: www.graspyouth.org
If you are struggling with gang involvement, or know someone who is, help is out there.This program works to prevent teens from joining gangs and helps them get out, too.

PUBLISHER'S NOTE TO EDUCATORS AND PARENTS:

All the websites featured above have been carefully reviewed to ensure that they are suitable for students. However, many websites change often, and we cannot guarantee that a site's future contents will continue to meet our high standards of educational value. Please be advised that students should be closely monitored whenever they access the Internet.

INDEX

ABOUT THE AUTHORS

Sarah Eason has authored many nonfiction books for children and has a special interest in health and social issues for young people. Karen Latchana Kenney is a well-known children's book author who has written a huge range information books for young people.